T0418589

Hug a Bug

Consultants

Ashley Bishop, Ed.D.

Sue Bishop, M.E.D.

Publishing Credits

Dona Herweck Rice, *Editor-in-Chief*

Robin Erickson, *Production Director*

Lee Aucoin, *Creative Director*

Tim J. Bradley, *Illustrator Manager*

Jason Peltz, *Illustrator*

Sharon Coan, *Project Manager*

Jamey Acosta, *Editor*

Rachelle Cracchiolo, M.A.Ed., *Publisher*

Teacher Created Materials

5301 Oceanus Drive

Huntington Beach, CA 92649-1030

http://www.tcmpub.com

ISBN 978-1-4333-2937-1

© 2012 Teacher Created Materials, Inc.

Printed in Malaysia

THU001.48806

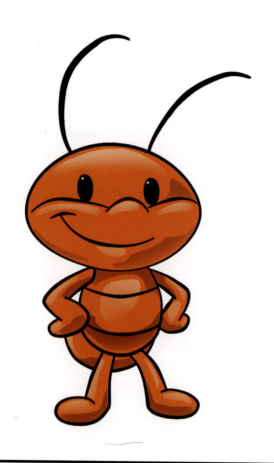

bug

I am a bug.

jug

I am in a jug.

mug

This is my mug.

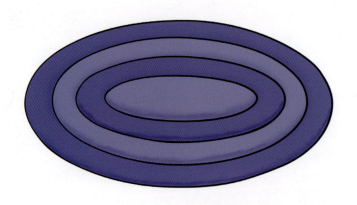

rug

This is my rug.

I like hugs!

Glossary

bug

hugs

jug

mug

rug

Sight Words

I   am

a   in

This   is

my   like

Extension Activities

Read the story together with your child. Use the discussion questions before, during, and after your reading to deepen your child's understanding of the story and the rime (word family) that is introduced.

The activities provide fun ideas for continuing the conversation about the story and the vocabulary that is introduced. They will help your child make personal connections to the story and use the vocabulary to describe prior experiences.

Discussion Questions
- Why would a bug be in a jug?
- Can a bug drink from a mug? Who drinks out of a mug?
- Do you like hugs? Who do you like to hug?

Activities at Home
- Look in your garden for different kinds of bugs. Have your child draw a picture of a bug.
- Make a list of as many -ug words as you can with your child. Have your child write a sentence using an -ug word.